THE BIG TEN

A QUICK-ACCESS GUIDE TO
TEN YOUTH MINISTRY ESSENTIALS

SCOTTY GIBBONS

SALUBRIS℠
RESOURCES

DEDICATION

This quick-access guide is dedicated to the heroic youth leaders who serve faithfully on the front lines. God is with you, and He will help you. My prayer is that He will use the nuggets in this book to make your job a little easier as you strive to present His love to a waiting generation.

CONTENTS

Introduction   7

CHAPTER 1   Leadership   9
              3 Keys to a Great Relationship With Your Leader

CHAPTER 2   Speaking   17
              5 Insights for Writing and Delivering Talks

CHAPTER 3   Pastoral Care   25
              14 Principles for Counseling, Weddings, & Funerals

CHAPTER 4   Campus Ministry   35
              3 Ideas for Impacting Local Schools

CHAPTER 5   Follow-Up   41
              *3 Steps for Helping Students Find Their Place in
              Your Ministry*

CHAPTER 6   Discipleship   47
              4 Thoughts on Helping Students Grow Spiritually

CHAPTER 7   Small Groups   55
              4 Steps to Making Small Groups a Big Deal

CHAPTER 8   Planning Events   63
              4 Keys to Gatherings That Hit the Mark

CHAPTER 9   Budget   73
              3 Insights for Making the Most of Any Budget

CHAPTER 10   Youth Leader Volunteers   81
              3 Insights for Building a Great Leadership Team

Appendices   91

Acknowledgments   121

About the Author   123

INTRODUCTION

You love God. You love students. You want to make a difference.

It's a simple calling, but it gets complicated when your passion to reach a generation collides with budgets, apathetic teens, disgruntled parents, and leaders with high expectations. It's no wonder most youth leaders throw in the towel during the first year.

It doesn't have to be that way, though. Help is available.

After more than two decades in student ministry, I've seen youth and their culture change, but the principles of healthy, effective ministry remain the same. In this little book, I want to share with you some of the thoughts, lessons, insights, and ideas I've learned along the way to help you become more effective in your calling.

This quick-access resource isn't meant to address every challenge you'll face in youth ministry, but my hope and prayer is that the field-tested, practical advice in the following pages will help you navigate the essentials—what I call the big ten! You'll find that all of the principles in these pages can be easily understood and easily applied. Whether you're a volunteer, a part-time youth leader, or a seasoned, full-time youth pastor, you'll want to keep this helpful resource close and refer to it often.

You don't need to go it alone. Let's do this together.

CHAPTER 1

LEADERSHIP

3 KEYS TO A GREAT
RELATIONSHIP WITH YOUR LEADER

TOP TIP *Make sure there's a clear understanding of how the lines of communication between you and your leader will flow on an ongoing basis.*

"No man is an island." The familiar adage applies to youth leaders, as well. You and your ministry exist within your local church. So it's important to understand the role of student ministry in the context of your church's overall mission. That starts with a shared understanding between you and your leader about your role and the role of the student ministry. I get that youth leaders are passionate about making a difference. You want to impact a school, change a community, reach a generation—take over the world! But most don't get excited about serving their leader. However as a youth leader, this is your primary role.

God's Word tells us to serve our leaders as if we're serving the Lord. As you do, keep these three critical keys in mind.

1. DISCOVER YOUR LEADER'S VISION AND MAKE IT YOUR OWN.

- ***God has called you to a person, not a place.*** As a youth leader, you aren't primarily called to a city or a school or a particular group of students. First and foremost, God has called you to serve your leader.

- ***Find out what's important to your leader and make it important to you.*** Engage and ask questions to discover where God is leading your leader and look for ways you can come alongside him/her to advance that vision. Your job is to get on your leader's page—not to get the leader on yours. If you're unclear about your leader's priorities, ask him/her. Don't make assumptions.

- ***The goals of your student ministry should work in conjunction with the church's mission.*** Work together with your leader and his/her team to identify and develop the role the student ministry will play in the church and community—and how that role will support the overall vision of the church. When your ministry is competing with, rather than complementing, the big-picture mission, you're off base.

- ***God blesses your obedience, not your brilliance.***
  There will be times when you disagree with your
  leader. And there will be times you may very well
  be right. But unless it's illegal or unbiblical, defer to
  your leader's direction. God's blessing comes with
  unity and a heart of submission. So even when you
  feel like you have a "better" idea, inform the leader
  of your perspective and then submit to, and support,
  his/her decision.

2. WORK HARD AT COMMUNICATING EFFECTIVELY WITH YOUR LEADER.

- ***Communicate in a timely manner.*** Ideally,
  before even accepting your role as a youth leader,
  communicate clearly about your job description and
  what's expected of you. If you've already started, yet
  still don't have clarity on your role, call a time-out and
  have that conversation sooner than later. If you delay,
  the mist of confusion will become a fog of frustration.
  When sharing a weighty matter with your leader, be
  sensitive to the timing. Right before the pastor speaks
  is not the best time to bring up an issue. You'll just
  add to his/her stress load. Waiting an hour until after
  service ends is a great way to serve him/her.

- ***Communicate consistently.*** Make sure there's a clear understanding of how the lines of communication will flow on an ongoing basis. Does your leader prefer the bulk of your conversations to take place via email or face-to-face? Once a week or once a month? In the absence of conversation, misunderstandings abound.

- ***Communicate honestly.*** If you don't know how to handle a situation, admit it. Don't cave to the pressure of pretending you have it all together. Eventually, time will reveal you don't. Most leaders would rather you take five minutes to ask a question than two hours explaining to them why you made a bad decision. If you're feeling overwhelmed and seriously wondering if you can carry your current load of responsibilities, talk with your leader. Speaking up now will help avoid future burnout.

- ***Communicate respectfully.*** There will be times when the conversations will be difficult. Perhaps you feel frustrated. It's appropriate to be honest about that. But speak the truth—in love. If there's a disagreement, seek first to understand, and then to be understood. Honor always wins.

3. KEEP YOUR LEADER APPRISED OF WHAT'S HAPPENING IN THE YOUTH MINISTRY—BOTH THE GOOD AND THE BAD.

- ***Celebrate the wins.*** Don't miss an opportunity to share a great report with your leaders. That's the stuff they're hoping and praying for in ministry.

- ***Tell your leader when there's a problem.*** It's human nature to want to share the highlights and hide the lowlights. In the long run, this kind of secrecy will work against you. Give your leader the opportunity to help problem-solve with you.

- ***Tell your leader about problems early on.*** Leaders don't like surprises. For example, if a problem involves a parent, let leadership hear about it from you—*before* hearing about it from the parent.

ASK YOURSELF

1. *What does my leader want to see happen in the lives of students and the student ministry in our church? In our community? Be specific!*

2. *What does success and a healthy ministry look like in this particular church environment? How will I know when I've hit the mark?*

3. *What three to five things can I do to communicate more consistently, honestly, and respectfully with my leader?*

CHAPTER 2

SPEAKING

5 INSIGHTS FOR WRITING AND DELIVERING TALKS

TOP TIP

Wrestle with the text until you're convinced the message is critical. If you're not gripped by its importance, you can be sure students won't be either.

Teaching students can be intimidating and overwhelming. Week after week, the task shows up on your "to do" list. Fortunately, there are things you can do to help reduce the pressure and actually make writing and speaking something you look forward to doing.

Consider these five insights before you tackle your next talk.

1. PREPARE AN ANNUAL SPEAKING CALENDAR.

- **Start with prayer.** Take a day to pray and plan for the upcoming year. If you're following an annual calendar, schedule time in December to pray and hear from God about your messages. If you're following a school calendar, set aside a day in July where you ask God to lead you as you map out the year's topics to be covered.

- **Make a list of topics.** List ideas you feel are important in helping students find and follow Jesus. It doesn't have to be a perfect list. Simply note any subject you consider critical for youth. Start with general ones (relationships, temptation, prayer).

- **Plan a message series.** Don't overestimate what students will retain from one talk and how much you can cover. Focusing on a topic for several weeks helps them to "get" it. Nor do you want your series to drag on and cause students to lose interest. Target three to four weeks. Try to write at least an outline for all of the talks in a series before you begin it. Knowing where you're going and how you're getting there will give you confidence to present each talk. A few weeks before you start a series, share about it and build anticipation for it.

- ***Begin to plug topics into a calendar.*** Start with topics that make sense seasonally. February is an ideal time to speak on relationships. Halloween provides plenty of context for addressing fears, darkness, etc. Easter is ideal for a series on the deity of Christ. Thanksgiving is great for dealing with gratitude. Christmas is perfect for a series on generosity. Placing topics around the appropriate times of the calendar year provides natural reinforcement for your talks. From there, you can begin to fill in the other dates with remaining topics.

2. MAKE SERMON PLANNING A TEAM EFFORT.

- ***Recruit a creative team.*** Identify a few trusted people, including students, to help determine your topics and discuss creative ways to present the talks.

- ***Meet quarterly to flesh out the topics you've outlined.*** This will allow you time to develop creative elements and media to support your sermon.

- ***Discuss ways to make the message memorable.*** Brainstorm titles and illustrations that will stick with the students and help them better understand and retain the truth you're presenting.

3. THINK ABOUT YOUR AUDIENCE AS YOU WRITE.

- ***Know who you're speaking to.*** Take time to consider
  any issues your students are currently dealing with
  (finals, graduation, a school tragedy, etc.).

- ***Know why this matters to them.*** Wrestle with the
  text until you're convinced the message is critical. If
  you're not gripped by its importance, you can be sure
  students won't be either.

- ***Don't assume students will be familiar with the
  Scripture and Bible illustrations you reference.*** Give
  them context. For example, "Paul used to persecute
  Christians before God showed up in his life ..."

4. FOCUS ON ONE MAIN POINT.

- ***Establish the big idea.*** Before you begin to craft
  your sermon, type the big idea at the top of the page.
  As you develop the message, keep your eye on the
  main thought to ensure you're staying on track.

- ***Guard the main idea.*** After you've finished writing,
  review your talk and look for other "points" or
  themes that may detract from the main one. If the

point or illustration doesn't reinforce the main idea, then don't use it.

- **Share the main idea with a friend.** Explain your main point to someone else before you present your talk and ask that person to explain it back to you. If they can't easily do that, you have more work to do.

5. YOUR MESSAGE SHOULD LEAD STUDENTS TO ACTION.

- **Answer the question "What does this look like in my life?"** Make sure students can connect the dots of your message to their everyday lives. Offer practical examples of how the topic might show up in their relationships, school day, etc.

- **Answer the question, "Now what?"** What's the next immediate step? The call to action must be easy both to understand and apply. Instead of simply urging students to "witness more," challenge them to choose three people to pray for and ask God to provide opportunities to start a spiritual conversation with these people.

UTILIZE A GUEST SPEAKER

Don't assume that you need to deliver the messages at your events—especially if you're doing a lot of the leadership and administrative aspects. Utilize another leader on your team who has a speaking gift. Or bring in a guest speaker for a special event or retreat. Deciding to hire a speaker doesn't have to mean a big expenditure or big name. Even a small youth group can probably afford to invite another nearby pastor to share the message(s). Or a local friend may be willing to do the job for just a small gesture of thanks. If you won't be able to provide a generous honorarium, communicate that when you extend the invitation. When you're at a retreat and busy trying to sort out room assignments and finalize activity details, you'll be relieved that you handed off the teaching.

Of course, if you have a team in place that has taken responsibility for much of the planning and you have something specific you want to say and prefer to do the teaching, that can be great too. Just make sure it's a conscious decision and not an afterthought because you failed to plan.

When considering an outside speaker, do your homework. Even if you know the leader on a personal level or have heard them speak at an event, make sure they match up with your group theologically and doctrinally.

And set up your speaker to win. Make sure expectations are clear ahead of time; discuss the goal of the service, the targeted length of the message, and the specific call to response.

ASK YOURSELF

1. *How can I do a better job of planning topic ideas and ensuring they resonate with students?*

2. *What are my next steps for putting together a creative planning team?*

3. *Do students come away knowing and grasping the main truth of the talk?*

4. *How am I challenging teens in specific ways to apply what they're learning?*

CHAPTER 3

PASTORAL CARE

14 PRINCIPLES FOR COUNSELING, WEDDINGS, AND FUNERALS

TOP TIP

Use Scripture as your guide. As a leader in a pastoral role, your job is to point students back to the Word of God.

Not all youth pastors are great at being pastoral. Some are more natural communicators, others are gifted administrators. But many are wired to be shepherds who are in their sweet spot when pastoring students. Whether or not the pastoral care aspects come naturally to you, they're essential in youth ministry. You may not face these issues every day, but when you do, few things will be as important to you and your students. Here are a few thoughts to set you up to win in these critical areas.

1. COUNSELING: DEVELOP A PLAN FOR TALKING WITH HURTING STUDENTS.

- ***Never promise to keep confidentiality.*** If you've been a youth leader for more than a month, you've probably had a student approach you and ask if he could share something with you and request that you not tell anyone. With good intentions, many youth leaders agree to keep the secret, wanting to be a safe and trusted friend. And in some cases, after hearing the situation you'll realize you have to get the student some help. Perhaps he is struggling with suicidal thoughts or opens up about abuse happening in his home. As a leader, you can't keep this kind of information confidential. Instead, when a student asks you to keep a secret, consider saying, "You can be sure I won't unnecessarily share your personal information with people. But if you need help, I'm committed to communicating with the appropriate people to give you the help you need."

- ***Use discretion for where and how long you counsel students.*** Having another leader with you for counseling sessions is ideal. If it's a situation where another leader isn't available, keep the conversation brief and always meet in a public setting. If you meet with a student two times and there's still a need for more sessions, at that point it's important to consider getting the student to a professional counselor.

- ***Limit the scope of your counseling.*** Unless you're a trained, professional counselor, don't try to tackle major problems on your own. Students battling addiction, self-harm, grief recovery, mental illness, and other serious challenges need to be referred to a professional counselor. You can pray with them and encourage them along the way, but resist the pressure to have all the answers. Have the courage and wisdom to admit when the situation is beyond your training.

- ***Use Scripture as your guide.*** As a leader in a pastoral role, your job is to point students back to the Word of God. Our message is not one of self-help. Our hope is in the power of God. Teach students to go to Scripture for wisdom on how to handle life's challenges.

2. WEDDINGS: DEVELOP A PLAN FOR RESPONDING TO THAT IMPORTANT QUESTION, "WILL YOU MARRY US?"

- ***Get the details before committing to marry a couple.*** There are obvious details like date and location. If the ceremony will be three hours away in another city, that's important information to know. Beyond that, are you comfortable being part of the ceremony if an additional minister from another religion also participate? Does your church require leadership to approve all music used in the ceremony? Some pastors won't perform the ceremony if both individuals aren't Christians. Others use it as a chance to share the gospel. Before you say, "Yes, I'll marry you," think through these questions and know what you will and won't do.

- **Make sure the couple receives pre-marital counseling.** You don't necessarily have to be the one who does the counseling, but it's critical they get it. These sessions together can be the greatest gift you provide this couple as they prepare to start their new journey.

- **Get to know the couple on a personal level.** In the event that you don't know both well, get to know them as much as possible. Weaving personal comments and stories into your message makes the ceremony much more meaningful. If you know very little about them when they ask you to officiate, you can still get to know them in a few meetings over coffee by just asking specific questions: What's their faith story? How did they meet? What was their first official date? Are there any funny or embarrassing stories from the dating period? What do they admire most about one another?

- **Make the ceremony special.** Work with the couple to write vows that will be meaningful to them. Ask if they prefer a contemporary feel or a more traditional approach. As you plan out the different aspects of the ceremony, pay attention to the flow and transitions between different segments. Fifteen minutes for the message and forty-five minutes for the entire ceremony are good targets.

- **Follow-up.** Put the outline of your sermon in a frame and send it to them on their one-year anniversary. A year later, the honeymoon is over and reality has set in. An encouraging word from you could be more helpful than you'll ever know.

3. FUNERALS: DEVELOP A PLAN FOR OFFERING PEACE AND COMFORT IN LIFE'S MOST DIFFICULT TRIALS.

- **Let God work through you to bring His comfort.** As you serve in ministry, there will be times you have the unfortunate responsibility and privilege to walk with families through the darkest of times. As difficult as those times may be, and as inadequate as you may feel to respond, God can use you in these dark days to bring comfort and healing when families need it most. They don't need a sermon or pat answers. They simply need your presence. But even trying to simply be there for a grieving family can be intimidating. Try going along with a seasoned minister to watch how they handle this responsibility.

- ***Respond quickly and appropriately.*** As soon as you hear that someone in your church has passed away, contact your pastor to make sure he's aware. Then make contact with the family and let them know you'd like to come see them. Be sensitive to the moment. Your goal is to be close without being an intrusion. Families and students will need your support in different ways based on their relationship with you. When the time is appropriate, let the family know the church stands ready to care for them. Offer to help with meals. Provide guidance for working with the funeral home. However, be careful to not over-promise what the church can do.

- ***Coordinate details with the funeral home.*** Make sure that everyone's plans for the funeral are in agreement. During times of grief, there can be miscommunication, which only adds to everyone's stress. Go over the details. If you're performing the ceremony, ask specific questions: Is there a graveside service? What are the expectations for music? Who will be participating in the service? Try to keep the service to less than an hour. Your sermon doesn't need to be more than fifteen minutes tops. You're responsible to make sure the service honors the deceased as well as the people who are there to remember that person. Make sure the ceremony does both.

- ***Make your message meaningful.*** Speak from God's Word. His Word is powerful and can bring supernatural peace. Speak words of comfort directly to the family. In many cases, it's difficult to know the true condition of someone's heart. Be careful to not give into the pressure of assuring people their loved one is in heaven. Leave that decision in God's hands. It's certainly appropriate to honor the person and to celebrate their life while on earth. But when it comes to your actual sermon, you're better off preaching to the living. Be sensitive to the moment and use discretion, but leverage this opportunity to share the hope of Christ with those present. People are often very open to thinking about eternity, and their own mortality, at a funeral. Give them Jesus.

- **Follow-up.** Set a reminder on your calendar to follow up with the family each year on the anniversary of their loved one's passing. Give them a call or send a card. Remembering their loss and taking some time to reminisce over some of the happy memories will be an ongoing source of comfort and strength.

ASK YOURSELF

1. *Have I set up healthy boundaries for counseling students? If not, what's my plan for knowing what I will and won't do?*

2. *Do I have a plan for working with a couple as we coordinate their big day?*

3. *Do I feel confident in how I would minister to a family during a time of loss?*

CHAPTER 4

CAMPUS MINISTRY

3 IDEAS FOR
IMPACTING LOCAL SCHOOLS

TOP TIP

Make a point to greet school leaders each time, even if it's a wave from a distance. Ministry flows out of relationships, and relationships take time. Be consistent and patient.

For youth leaders, the local junior high schools and high schools are your mission field. But how that looks for you and your ministry may be very different than how it plays out for other leaders and campuses. If principals and staff know you and welcome you, great! But how much campus access you have isn't the measure of success. Instead, focus your energy on what you can control: serving and impacting schools and their students in helpful ways. As you look for ways to come alongside your local campuses, consider these three ideas.

1. START BY BUILDING TRUST.

- **Introduce yourself to the leadership.** When possible, let a teacher or coach you know make a personal introduction.

- **Support school events.** As much as possible, attend sporting events, concerts, and plays. Make a point to greet school leaders each time, even if it's a wave from a distance. Keep it short and sweet but always try to connect. Ministry flows out of relationships, and relationships take time. Be consistent and patient.

- **Find a need the school has and meet it.** Watch for opportunities to serve. Pick up trash after a game. Help raise funds for the computer lab. Perhaps your church could take a day in the summer to help clean, paint, or repair the school's building. Proverbs says that the gift makes way for the giver. A simple renovation of the teacher's lounge will speak volumes to school staff as they see you support the school and its leadership with no strings attached.

2. TRAIN YOUR STUDENTS AS CAMPUS MISSIONARIES.

- ***Explain the biblical mandate.*** Equip your students with a biblical understanding of evangelism. Remind teens that, as Christ-followers, the only reason they're still here on earth is to share the hope they've found with those who need it.

- ***Take the fear out of witnessing.*** Help students see that sharing Christ can be natural and doesn't have to be weird. Living a life that honors Christ, coupled with conversations that share their personal story of faith, can have a powerful impact.

- ***Eliminate the fear of failure.*** Students shouldn't carry the burden of converting anyone. Only God can do that. Help them to see the power of simply starting a spiritual conversation and then celebrate those stories. Sometimes we plant seeds. Other times, we water them. But only God transforms a life. Remind them of that truth.

3. HOST SCHOOL-RELATED EVENTS.

- ***Meet at the church.*** Throw a back-to-school community event and give local administrators an opportunity to share their hearts and vision for the district. Publicly honor them and reaffirm your desire to support them in whatever way possible. If you host any type of community event, do it well. Represent God's kingdom with excellence.

- **Meet in the gym.** After football games, invite students to "fifth quarter" events and show a highlight video of that night's game on a large screen. Provide food and giveaways. The atmosphere should be fun and high-energy. A crowd attracts a crowd, so work with other churches to have students arrive early. Be careful to not damage any school property, and make a special effort to leave the facilities better off than you found them. You want school leaders to approve your future requests.

- **Meet in the office.** During National Teachers Appreciation Week, bring in fresh bagels, doughnuts, and good coffee one morning with a thank-you card to teachers. Go the extra mile and include office staff and workers who are often overlooked.

ASK YOURSELF

1. *What steps will I take to build trust with local school leaders?*

2. *How can we practically serve our local schools?*

3. *What school-related events can we host as a church?*

4. *Do our students see themselves as missionaries to their campuses? How can we do a better job of inspiring, challenging, and equipping them to share the hope of Jesus?*

CHAPTER 5

FOLLOW-UP

3 STEPS FOR HELPING STUDENTS FIND THEIR PLACE IN YOUR MINISTRY

TOP TIP

Be intentional about connecting a visitor with an outgoing student in your ministry who will make the visitor feel at home. Students would rather go to a boring youth service with friends than to the coolest service alone.

In youth ministry, we've become pros at drawing a crowd, but we're not nearly as good at closing the back door. It's exciting to lead people to Jesus, but going with them on their journey filled with ups and downs is not nearly as enjoyable. And how intentional are we about finding out why a student who used to be very involved in the life of the church is now nowhere to be found? Follow-up is all about connection. As you work through your follow-up strategy, consider these three thoughts on connecting students.

1. DEVELOP A PLAN FOR CONNECTING WITH NEW STUDENTS WHO COME TO YOUR MINISTRY.

- ***Focus on first impressions.*** Follow-up with first-time guests begins the moment they walk through your doors. Take time to consider the first impression your youth ministry makes. It's easy to allow familiarity with your ministry to cloud your perception and, as a result, not really grasp how fresh eyes see your events. You never get a second chance to make a first impression, so make the most of it.

- ***Connect students to students.*** Be intentional about connecting a visitor with an outgoing student in your ministry who will make that new person feel at home. Students would rather go to a boring youth service with friends than to the coolest service alone. Work hard to connect them relationally. Don't assume that just because you make an introduction, students will naturally hit it off and become best friends. Look for connecting points (the school they both attend, an activity they both participate in) when you make the introduction.

- ***Empower students to follow up with students.***
  Instill in your students a sense of responsibility to
  not only invite others to a youth event but also to
  follow up and invite them to check out a small group.

- ***Reach out to the family.*** Follow up with parents
  of visitors within twenty-four hours. Provide
  information about your ministry and any upcoming
  events. Offer to answer any questions they may have.
  Your best shot at ministering to a visiting student is
  including their family.

2. DEVELOP A PLAN FOR GROWING STUDENTS WHO COME TO CHRIST.

- ***Prepare new believers for reality.*** Be honest with
  new believers about the difficulties that are still
  present even after surrendering to Christ. They will
  quickly realize that life's problems haven't gone away.
  They may actually find life more difficult on some
  levels.

- ***Assure new believers they're not alone.*** The student
  may not get a lot of support from family or friends
  about their decision to follow Christ. Make sure they
  know they can contact you or other leaders anytime
  they have doubts or questions, or just need to talk.

- ***Explain next steps.*** Provide specific and practical next steps and explain how beneficial it is to follow them. Explain what water baptism is all about and why it's important. Provide a simple Bible reading plan designed for new believers and offer for a leader to go through it with them. Connect them with a small group where they can be encouraged by other students (more on small groups in chapter 7).

3. DEVELOP A PLAN FOR CONNECTING STUDENTS TO A SERVING OPPORTUNITY.

- ***Create or use a system for tracking students' involvement.*** Put a system in place to identify when students start to fade away or struggle to get involved. The larger your ministry grows, the more difficult this becomes.

- ***Discover why a student stopped coming.*** Contact the student personally to ask why they aren't coming anymore. This will be invaluable information. Sometimes it may be hard to hear, but you need to know the truth.

- ***Problem-solve.*** Determine if there's anything you can do to bring the student back. If so, do it!

- ***Make follow-up a team effort.*** Enlist small group leaders and other youth volunteers to help shepherd students. Teach student leaders how to reach out to students who are no longer coming. For many churches, one of the largest mission fields is sitting in the Sunday morning service.

- ***Help students find a place to serve.*** A student who's involved in serving is much more apt to stay plugged into the life of the church.

ASK YOURSELF

1. *Do newcomers feel welcome and wanted in our youth ministry?*

2. *What is my plan for following up with newcomers and new believers? Is this plan working? Why or why not?*

3. *What system are we using to track when someone stops coming to the group?*

CHAPTER 6

DISCIPLESHIP

4 THOUGHTS ON HELPING STUDENTS GROW SPIRITUALLY

Challenge students to immerse themselves in God's Word to discover the life He's calling them to. Teach teens that discipleship is really just about regularly taking steps to know Jesus more.

In our culture, there's often a difference between calling yourself a Christian and considering yourself a disciple. The Bible offers no such distinction. Nonetheless, in many youth ministries we work hard to see a student buy into the idea of being a Christian and then consider it gravy if that student actually commits to deepening that walk by truly following in the footsteps of Jesus. Our job as youth leaders is not to add to the number of those who claim Christianity as their

6 DO'S AND DON'TS OF DISCIPLESHIP

DO pursue students for deeper relationship.

DON'T smother.

DON'T leave students feeling abandoned.

DO connect teens with leaders willing to invest in them.

DON'T treat students like a project or an obligation.

DO show them what it means to follow Jesus
by the way you live your life.

---

religion, but to make true disciples—fully devoted followers of Christ. As you process how to go about that, focus in on these four thoughts.

1. GIVE STUDENTS A BIBLICAL UNDERSTANDING OF DISCIPLESHIP.

- ***Start at salvation.*** When you present the gospel, provide students with a scriptural basis for what it truly means to follow Jesus. While we often mistakenly see discipleship as something that occurs post-salvation, help students understand that outside of a total surrender of self and complete embracing of the cross, there is no salvation.

- ***Use each message and event to reinforce authentic relationship with God.*** Draw students' attention to the differences between American "consumer" Christianity and biblical Christianity. Challenge them to immerse themselves in God's Word and to discover the life He's calling them to. Start small. Teach teens that discipleship is really just about regularly taking steps to know Jesus more.

- ***Teach dependency on Christ.*** Students often get discouraged when they realize there's still a battle with sin nature even after salvation. Train students to understand that spiritual growth is not about personal perfection but the spiritual direction of their lives. The same grace that saves them sustains them.

- ***Cultivate a hunger for Jesus.*** As youth leaders, we have to work diligently to ensure students aren't unintentionally developing a stronger bond with the youth ministry than with Christ. Be intentional about training students first and foremost to pursue God and then allow life's priorities and passions to flow from there. When we make church attendance, ministry involvement, and behavior modification the goals, we've strayed from God's plan for discipleship.

2. CREATE SIMPLE PLANS FOR SPIRITUAL GROWTH.

- ***Make prayer easy.*** Help students see that prayer is not a formula or a spiritual ritual by which we make God happy or relieve a guilty conscience. Prayer is an ongoing conversation with the One who made us—the One who loves us and wants to guide us toward fulfillment that can only be found in Him. The more time we spend in conversation with God, the more we capture His heart and discover His ways. Challenge teens to set a daily goal to talk to Jesus and to listen to Him.

- ***Direct students toward helpful Bible reading plans.*** Ask them to spend a few minutes each day reading the Bible. Explain how reading Scripture is the primary way God talks to us. Providing an easily understood translation, and passages appropriate for younger Christians, will help them avoid discouragement, and instead will create a pattern of listening to God. The more time they spend in God's Word, the more familiar they will become with His voice.

- ***Encourage students to journal.*** Writing about what they're reading will help them process what they're learning. It will also provide encouragement and perspective in the future when they look back and see God's faithfulness in their spiritual journey.

3. OFFER VARYING LEVELS OF CLASSES OR SMALL GROUPS.

- ***Have a comprehensive plan.*** Determine how you'll take a new believer through the process of growing at different levels. Think through what you'd like a graduating senior to know about their faith when exiting your student ministry—and develop a plan to get them there.

- ***Study a topic.*** Some spiritual growth opportunities can be centered around topics: a class on relationships, knowing God's will, or starting spiritual conversations with others. Topics like discovering and developing God-given talents are fun to study and easy to apply. When choosing your topic, keep the gender, age and spiritual maturity of the group in mind.

- ***Go through a book of the Bible.*** Select a book of the Bible to go through as a class on Sunday mornings. For younger Christians, Proverbs or James would be great places to start. If you have a group of seniors who have already gone through multiple levels of discipleship with you, consider a study on Acts or Romans.

- ***Read a faith-building book.*** Consider reading a book as a group and discussing it together. Again, keep age, gender, and spiritual maturity in mind. But don't be afraid to challenge their thinking. Perhaps a group could benefit from a journey that causes them to think through what they believe and why they believe it.

4. BUILD MENTORING RELATIONSHIPS.

- ***Spend time doing life with students.*** Relational discipleship is the most effective approach you can take. Trust is built, experiences are shared, and spiritual growth occurs. Invite students into your life. Give them the opportunity to see firsthand what it's like to follow God and worship Him in everyday life.

- ***Allow students to see your own ups and downs.*** Don't hide your flaws. Teens will learn how to struggle with doubt and wrestle with faith without abandoning it. When appropriate, let them know what you're working through in your own walk with God.

- **Pay attention to the highs and lows in students' lives.** Send an encouraging text when they win and send them two when they lose! If they're going through a difficult time, assure them they aren't going through it alone. Don't smother them, but be there.

- **Don't be afraid of tough questions.** And don't stifle students from asking them. Encourage this. Work through the answers together. This process will grow their faith much more than a canned textbook response.

ASK YOURSELF

1. *What is my plan for discipling our students?*

2. *Have I created enough quick-access entry points for teens?*

3. *How will I accommodate the wide range of spiritual maturity among these students?*

4. *What do I want my students' spiritual lives to look like when they graduate from this student ministry?*

CHAPTER 7

SMALL GROUPS

4 STEPS TO MAKING SMALL GROUPS A BIG DEAL

TOP TIP *Don't be afraid to ask people to get involved as leaders. And don't feel guilted into putting a willing-but-not-able body into a role that isn't the right fit just because you need leaders.*

Small groups can seem deceptively easy to manage: Split up the students by age, geographic area, school, or gender; find a church member willing to open their home; and recruit a leader who can follow whatever latest, new youth curriculum you ordered online—and you're good to go. However, as with most areas of ministry, great small groups don't just happen; they take planning. Think through what your students need most right now and what will best serve your ministry at this point. As you do, remember these four steps.

1. FIND AND DEVELOP THE RIGHT LEADERS.

- ***Ask God for help.*** If you aren't able to lead the small group, or have numerous groups and thus need more leaders, pray for God to send the right people your way.

- ***Watch for potential leaders.*** If you notice someone is a good communicator, shows leadership potential, or seems to love hosting, schedule a time to get together to talk about possible opportunities. Don't be afraid to ask people to get involved. And don't feel guilted into putting a willing-but-not-able body into a role that isn't the right fit just because you need leaders.

- ***Train group leaders to lead well.*** Develop small group leaders to help teens connect relationally. A good leader will facilitate rather than hijack the conversation. They also will know how to handle it when a student is dominating a discussion, or how to engage one who is reluctant to talk. An annual training event is helpful, but ongoing training is a must. Keep your small group leaders informed and encouraged.

- ***Equip group leaders to win.*** Provide leaders with quality curriculum or notes for the topic to be covered; and do so in a timely manner. If it's video-based, make sure they watch it in advance and have predetermined questions for the discussion. Games and ideas for icebreakers are invaluable to leaders attempting to engage students. Make sure they have all they need.

2. DECIDE WHEN AND WHERE TO MEET.

- ***Get creative with group meeting times.*** Many senior high students are swamped with school, homework, sports, and extracurricular activities. Finding a workable meeting time for some students can be challenging. If school nights and weekends aren't options, consider a breakfast group before school. If possible, help students set up a group during the lunch period. You won't be able to accommodate everyone, but offering multiple options positions you to reach more students.

- ***Consider the age group and the goal of the study when deciding on a location.*** Is it more of an activity-based group or more of a Bible study? Junior high, senior high, or both? When setting a time and place for junior high small groups, work to make it easy for parents to pick up students. Always ending on time will be greatly appreciated by parents who are trying to wrap up their day. Meeting at the church when parents are already there seems to work best for most junior high groups. Senior high groups tend to do better off-site in host homes. There's no perfect size for a small group, but finding a venue that fits the size and context of your group is essential. Ideally, shoot for each group to run between ten and twenty students.

3. CREATE AN ATMOSPHERE FOR RELATIONSHIP BUILDING AND BIBLE STUDY.

- *Make it a fun, welcoming place.* Whether meeting in a room in the church or in a host home, encourage host leaders to warmly greet each student by name when he/she walks in the door. Create a welcoming atmosphere with appropriate music, lighting, drinks and snacks, and comfortable seating. When selecting the music and snacks, encourage leaders to cater to the students' interests, not their own personal preference.

- ***Make it an effective space.*** A small group of twelve meeting in a two-hundred-seat auditorium is a leader's nightmare; so is a group of twenty-eight people in a ten-by-ten living room. A fairly full room with a little space to grow is ideal. Pay attention to the seating arrangement. You should be able to see the eyes of each student. And six girls crammed into a two-person loveseat *will* limit the length of your discussion. As the facilitator, try to avoid sitting with your back to the entrance to the room—this will reduce the distractions of people entering and exiting.

4. APPRECIATE GROUP HOSTS AND THEIR HOMES.

- ***Clearly share expectations with hosts.*** Before asking host families to commit, communicate thoroughly with them. Their homes are about to be invaded by a group of teenagers. When it comes to respecting other people's property, some of these students have been trained less than others. While leaders and students should do everything possible to care for the home, it's wise to acknowledge up front that teens will be teens. Discuss who will be responsible for food. To lighten the load of the host home, create a hospitality team when possible.

Establish firm start and end dates so that hosts know what they're committing to.

- **Honor hosts' homes.** Make sure the day of the week and meeting times work for the family before you promote those dates and times to students. Ask group leaders to talk to the host ahead of time for house specifics, such as parking, the host's policy on shoes in the house, and where food is and isn't allowed. Make sure group leaders communicate these rules to students, so there are no surprises. If something breaks or is damaged, offer to repair or replace the item. Make sure the hosts have help enforcing the end time and clearing out stragglers.

- **Express your appreciation.** Occasionally send thank-you notes to hosts with details of how their service is impacting specific students. Share stories with them of individuals who've experienced life-change as a result of the small group ministry. At the end of the season, provide a nice gift from the group (for example, a one-time professional housecleaning) along with specific notes of thanks from the students.

ASK YOURSELF

1.   *What are the ministry goals of our small groups?*

2.   *When and where will they meet?*

3.   *What can we do to improve how we train small group leaders and set them up to win?*

4.   *How well have we communicated with our hosts?*

5.   *How will we show appreciation to our hosts for opening their homes?*

CHAPTER 8

PLANNING EVENTS

4 KEYS TO GATHERINGS THAT HIT THE MARK

If the purpose of your event is to introduce students to Christ, everything you do should support that goal. The entire night should work toward that point of decision.

Youth leaders are typically strong in the relational department. And we all understand the importance of being pastoral. But to most leaders, administration doesn't sound fun or spiritual! However, you'll never lead a healthy student ministry without paying attention to the details that keep the train moving. When planning events that will hit the mark and accomplish your goals, consider these four steps.

1. DEFINE YOUR GOAL.

- **Be intentional.** Is your event meant to be a fun, relational connection? Or do you want an event that provides a spiritual experience? The goal of your gathering should determine when, where, and how you plan and lead your event.

- **Be balanced.** Leaders tend to lead based on their individual personalities, which means we all need to guard against building a ministry that over-emphasizes any one aspect. Fun activities are terrific, community outreach is wonderful, and deep discussions of Scripture are important. But make sure that all of your events work together to accomplish your big-picture goal. A balanced schedule of events will help you work toward overall health for your ministry.

2. DEVELOP A PLAN.

- **Pick a date.** Once you've determined what kind of event you want to have, decide on a date. Don't just consult your own calendar; be sure to check the church calendar and local school calendars before committing. You don't want to go to the trouble of planning a great weekend only to find out there's a major conflict and no one can come.

- **_Choose a location._** Don't underestimate the importance of a great venue. The right location can make or break your event. Consider these questions when choosing a retreat location:

  1. *Is the price low enough that most students can afford it?*

  2. *Is the place available for your chosen dates?*

  3. *Do they have enough space to accommodate your group (not just for sleeping but also for meetings, activities, and meals)?*

  4. *Does the meeting setup meet your speaker and worship band's needs?*

  5. *How is the noise level? Will other groups be making noise when you're trying to meet? Will your group be expected to be quiet during free time to accommodate other groups?*

  6. *Are meals provided, or will you have to bring your own food or plan to eat out?*

- **_Make a checklist._** Think through all areas and make an action step for every task that needs to be accomplished before, during, and after the event. Assign a task to a person and put a deadline beside each item. No task is too small. Instead of having one line for "transportation," consider breaking it down like this:

Call and get prices for vans	Candice	September 5
Reserve vans	Kelly	September 12
Pick up vans	Bria	November 9
Drive vans to retreat	Allison	November 9
Return vans	Angel	November 10

- ***Put together a schedule.*** Make sure the schedule works toward your original purpose for the event. If your goal is a fun outing to build relationships, don't drive eight hours round trip for three hours at the theme park. If your goal is to present Christ at an event, make sure you're not spending 95 percent of your time on the fun and creative aspects and then trying to squeeze in a gospel presentation in the final few minutes. Keeping your purpose in mind, think through the flow of the event and keep things moving toward the goal.

PRESENTING CHRIST AT EVENTS

The best way to share Jesus is relationally from student to student. But offering events that give students an opportunity to invite a friend who's exploring their faith can be a great tool as well. As you consider how to use an event to provide a clear gospel presentation, consider the following steps:

- **Present the problem and the solution.** Until students rightly understand the problem of sin, they will not appreciate the offer of a Savior. Allow them to wrestle with the truth of their own sinfulness. Then share the great news of God's amazing grace.

- **Use illustrations appropriately.** There's nothing wrong with telling an emotional story. But remember the goal isn't to guilt students, shame them, or scare them into a decision. Let the story reinforce the scriptural point, not distract from it. There's also nothing wrong with using a token or movie clip illustration, but again, make sure it doesn't work against your attempt to urge students to think deeply about what God is speaking through His Word.

- **Give a clear and understandable call to respond.** The real win is not for students to raise their hand, sign a card, or even simply to pray a prayer. Rather, the goal is for a student to give sincere thought and wholehearted response to what God is calling them to do. So allow the Holy Spirit to work. Give students a moment to process. Then clearly communicate what it means to surrender their hearts to Christ, or take the next step in response to the challenge from Scripture.

---

3. GIVE STUDENTS OWNERSHIP.

- *Solicit input.* Involving students in the planning process allows them to have skin in the game. They may or may not like your creative ideas for the event's fun elements, but you can be certain they'll like the ones they come up with.

- *Delegate responsibility.* Give students as much of a role in planning and running the event as possible. Obviously, there are times where your purpose of the event would preclude them serving. A great event isn't just for students, but one that actually involves them.

4. EVALUATE YOUR EVENTS.

- ***Ask students for feedback.*** A casual way to discover what students thought about something is to ask what them what they enjoyed most. Comparing their responses will provide a good sampling for what was well received and what wasn't. A more formal approach could be to enlist a focus group, go through each aspect of the event, and get feedback.

- ***Ask volunteer leaders for feedback.*** What stood out to them? Your leaders will be able to speak more to the administrative aspects and organizational systems. If you should have allowed more time for check-in, write it down. If they make suggestions on how to better plan meal times, make a note. The more you do this, the better trained your leaders will become in providing helpful feedback. You don't want to cultivate a culture of criticism or perfectionism, but leaders who are constantly thinking of ways to improve your events are invaluable.

- ***Keep good notes.*** Record all observations good or bad. Include any new ideas that could take things up a notch next time. Keep the notes organized and easily accessible for when you begin to plan the next event. Keeping detailed notes will not only help

ensure you don't repeat mistakes but will also keep
you in a mindset of improvement.

ASK YOURSELF

1. *What type of event do I want to have in order to
    accomplish my specific goals?*

2. *Is our location conducive to the types of activities we
    want to offer and the time of year we plan to visit?*

3. *What is our plan to evaluate our events and improve in
    the future?*

CHAPTER 9

BUDGET

3 INSIGHTS FOR MAKING THE MOST OF ANY BUDGET

TOP TIP

Don't use your lack of resources as an excuse for a lack of impact. Having limited resources requires creativity and ingenuity that would otherwise be lost.

For any youth leader, budgeting comes down to stewardship. I realize it's easy to get distracted by what you don't have and what others do have, but God will provide what you need to carry out His plan. Don't ever blame a lack of funds for what you're not accomplishing in ministry. Instead, focus on being a good steward of what you do have and planning efficiently. No matter how small your budget, strive to be faithful with a few things, knowing that if you are, God will give you even more. As you do, focus on these three critical insights.

1. BE GRATEFUL FOR WHAT YOU HAVE.

- ***Focus on the resources available to you.*** While some churches invest financially in their youth programs, most youth leaders have to raise the bulk of whatever budget they use for ministry. This constant burden can become discouraging. Instead of focusing on what you don't have, be grateful for what you do have.

- ***Avoid the comparison trap.*** Don't compare your resources to what another church or ministry has. Remember that large ministries with big budgets had humble beginnings and that big budgets don't necessarily lead to effective ministry.

- ***Don't use your lack of resources as an excuse for a lack of impact.*** Often times, the greatest ministry ideas require the smallest budgets. Having limited resources requires creativity and ingenuity that would otherwise be lost. Little is much when God is in it.

2. BE WISE WITH HOW YOU SPEND.

- ***Do your homework.*** Before building your budget for an event or approaching a leader to request funds, make sure you have all of the information. Have you included accessories, taxes, and shipping and handling charges? Make sure you calculate *all* related costs. Doing your homework also means taking a little extra time to simply compare prices. Or if you're planning a trip that will require a hotel, try to go in off-peak times. Since you're reserving multiple rooms, ask for a group rate. Up-front planning can save you lots in the end.

- ***Remember that great events don't make up for lousy stewardship.*** Just because your event was a hit doesn't justify unwise spending. As excited as your leadership may be when they hear great reports of your canoe trip, that celebration will be tempered if they discover you went over budget by $300. God blesses us when we faithfully steward what He gives us, not when we impress heaven with our great event.

- ***Set up good systems.*** Utilize software or accounting systems your church already has in place to keep good records, file receipts, and track spending. The simplest rule to keep in mind when budgeting is to estimate income low and expense high. And if you commit to always spending less than you take in, you'll be in good shape.

- ***Prioritize your spending.*** With a limited amount of funds, where you spend each dollar needs to be very intentional. Determine what's most important and guard against losing your dollars to lesser priorities. If you charge students $50 per person to attend pizza and game night, you'll be able to purchase some killer prizes. But you'll also likely price most of the students right out of the event. And at the end of the event, it will be mission *un*-accomplished.

3. BE ACCOUNTABLE FOR HOW YOU SPEND.

- ***Begin with a clear understanding of what's available to you.*** It's difficult to own a responsibility if you don't first understand it. If you have no budget, ask about your parameters for raising funds. Are you free to solicit parents who can help invest? Do you have permission to solicit area businesses? If so, which ones? And how?

- ***Establish healthy communication regarding the budget.*** It's always good to have clear communication with your leader, but when it comes to money you need to put the information in writing and make extra sure that you and your leadership are on the same page. Will you have monthly budget meetings? How will you communicate budget questions or fundraising ideas?

- ***Serve your leadership by stewarding any resources well.*** One of the greatest ways you can honor your leader is by responsibly managing the church's resources. Mishandling the budget puts your leader in a difficult place with the board and adds unnecessary stress to his/her job. When you consistently come in under budget due to wise and responsible spending, your leadership will become more and confident in trusting you with church funds. When you're faithful with a few things, you'll be entrusted with more.

ASK YOURSELF

1.   *Do I have a clear understanding of how much is in my budget and when I can spend it? If there is no budget, do I have an understanding with my leadership of how I will ask for funds, or what parameters exist for me to raise a budget?*

2.   *What can I do better to track spending and turn in receipts, invoices, and other expenditures on time?*

3.   *Do I overspend and then try to justify it by talking about the ministry impact?*

4.   *Do I often compare our student ministry budget with another church's?*

5.   *Does my leadership know me as one who's responsible and effective with what I'm given? What can I do to build greater trust?*

CHAPTER 10

YOUTH LEADER VOLUNTEERS

3 KEYS FOR BUILDING
A GREAT LEADERSHIP TEAM

Spend time getting to know the heart of a potential leader before officially bringing them on the team. The better you know them, the better chance you'll have of placing them in the right role where they can have the greatest impact.

It's pretty common for youth leaders to feel overwhelmed. There are more needs than you can possibly meet this side of eternity. You care so much; you want to do so much; but the reality is there is only *so* much that you *alone* can do. Even if you're just starting with a handful of students, the only way you can move the ministry toward health and growth is by developing a team of leaders who will work together with you. Easier said than done. But don't be discouraged. It *is* possible to find quality volunteers to serve alongside you. It just takes time, perseverance, and intentionality. As you build your leadership team, remember these three keys.

1. RECRUIT GREAT LEADERS TO JOIN YOUR TEAM.

- ***Constantly recruit.*** As you meet new people and interact with individuals in your church, watch for potential leaders who may be a good addition to your team. Take advantage of every opportunity to share how God is working in the hearts of students. Tell stories of how God has used other leaders to bring changes to the lives of students who desperately needed it. Help people see how they also could be used by God to bring hope to students.

- ***Choose character over charisma.*** We're tempted to go after potential leaders who have a lot of personality or natural talent. And while there's nothing wrong with charisma, character is infinitely more important. Leaders of varying levels of spiritual maturity can certainly be a part of the team. Just make sure that you put them in appropriate roles. You wouldn't want a brand new convert to be the guy leading the Bible study on spiritual growth. And differing levels of talent will be present on every team. God isn't limited by our gift set. Just remember that skill can be taught, but spiritual character and a deep love for God are musts.

- ***Provide easy on-ramps and off-ramps.*** Offer opportunities for potential leaders to experience the heart of the student ministry in easy and safe ways. When they're exploring whether or not to get involved, give them short-term serving experiences that don't require a long-term commitment. Invite them to help out at an event to see the ministry in action. Follow up with them after the event to express appreciation and to ask if they'd be interested in getting involved at a deeper level. Be patient and allow God to stir their hearts. He's a much better recruiter than we are.

- ***Get to know potential leaders before putting them on the team.*** We often move too hastily in giving team members roles of influence. Spend time getting to know the heart of a potential leader before officially bringing them on the team. The better you know them, the better chance you'll have of placing them in the right role where they can have the greatest impact. If you ever feel uneasy about a leader seeking to get involved, pause. Have the courage to put the process on hold until you feel you've settled any concerns. Remember it's easier to move forwards than backwards. It's easier to hire than to fire. Always do background checks on leaders before allowing them to serve in your youth ministry, and check with your state to make sure you're meeting all legal expectations for proper screening.

- ***Call people to a great commitment.*** While you certainly don't want to pressure people to get involved, don't be reluctant to ask leaders to make a strong investment at the appropriate time. Too often, we soften the significance of what we're asking potential leaders to do, in fear that we may scare them off. But people want to be a part of something big, something that matters. Great leaders respond to great causes.

2. TRAIN LEADERS CONTINUALLY.

- ***Begin with orientation.*** Before a leader begins to serve, provide a thorough orientation about the DNA of your ministry. Help them to understand your priorities. Consider offering a personality test or gift assessment to help leaders find the right place to serve. Provide clear expectations for what you're asking them to do.

- ***Meet monthly.*** A brief meeting once a month provides a great venue for ongoing training and encouragement. Use this time to grow your leaders spiritually and to provide leadership lessons on ministering to students. Tackle topics that leaders are facing, like how to deal with students disrupting service, how to engage students in discussion at small group meetings, how to handle it when students share confidential information, etc. This is also a great time to problem-solve with your team and help them work through any challenges they're encountering. A monthly meeting is one of the strongest ways not only to develop your team, but also to ensure they stay encouraged and on mission.

- ***Gather annually.*** Once a year, plan a special day in January to celebrate the victories from the past year and share vision for the next one. It's critically important that leaders be reminded they're making a difference. A highlight video showing some of the moments from key events provides a great reminder of how God worked. Or consider having a few students share stories of how they were impacted. Then cast a vision for where you believe God is leading the ministry for the next year. Perhaps you'll use a theme for the year as a rallying point for services and events. This annual meeting is a perfect time for current team members to renew their commitment to the ministry or to go to a deeper level of service. It's also an ideal time for potential new leaders to come check out the ministry.

3. LEAD THEM EFFECTIVELY.

- ***Lead by example.*** Don't expect a committed team if you aren't a committed leader. Model servanthood. Demonstrate loyalty by the way you honor your leader. Be a generous person. Be gracious. As the leader, you set the tone for the ministry. You teach what you know, but you reproduce who you are.

- ***Provide the resources they need.*** Don't give leaders responsibility without resourcing them with the tools to get it done. If they're going to lead a small group, give them a great curriculum. Always set your leaders up to win.

- ***Create a culture of improvement.*** No ministry is perfect. And all leaders make mistakes. But healthy ministries are committed to improving. No matter how badly an event goes, you can take notes and look forward to doing better next time. No matter how great it goes, you can always find ways to take it up a notch the next time. Help your team members see areas where they can improve. Challenge them to not only identify weaknesses but to be solution-driven. Remember that what you reward gets repeated. You create the culture of your ministry by what you celebrate.

- *Share the glory and own the blame.* As the leader, there will be times you get more credit than you deserve. Other times, you will get more than your fair share of the blame. It just comes with your role. Endear yourself to your team by being quick to share the accolades with those who helped get the team win. And if something doesn't go so well, don't point fingers. Own the issue and work to do better in the future.

- *Deal with difficult leaders immediately.* If you have a leader who is causing problems, address the issue as soon as possible. Be careful not to assume the worst or jump to conclusions. Give them the benefit of the doubt, but have an honest conversation as soon as possible. Seek first to understand and then to be understood. If a person is off-mission, or is disrespecting you as a leader, meet with that person and do your best to work it out. If you can't resolve the issue, you need to make the tough call of asking the volunteer to step down. Make sure your church leadership is aware of the situation and supports your decision before you carry it out.

- ***Focus on relationships.*** Ministry flows out of relationships, and relationships take time. Be intentional about cultivating a relational community. Ministry isn't about programs, sermons, or trips. It's about people. Don't merely delegate tasks. Be a relational leader. Care more about your team members as friends than as workers.

- ***Encourage your leaders.*** Never miss an opportunity to say thanks. Let your leaders know when you notice them going the extra mile. And if you sense them getting discouraged, speak life into them. Perhaps a leader has been reaching out to a student who isn't responding. Encourage the leader never to give up. Assure him that God is working in ways we can't see. Send leaders handwritten notes from time to time. Catch them doing things right and cheer them on.

ASK YOURSELF

1. *How could I improve my process for identifying and actively recruiting volunteers?*

2. *How do I plan to train my youth ministry team?*

3. *What am I doing to keep our volunteers encouraged, equipped, and informed?*

4. *Do our volunteers understand the overall vision for our ministry and the students in it?*

5. *Would our volunteer leaders say they felt encouraged by me and through the work they're doing?*

APPENDICES

GO-TO RESOURCES

APPENDIX A

QUICK-ACCESS GUIDE TO SCRIPTURES FOR STUDENT MINISTRY TOPICS AND ISSUES

As a youth leader and authority figure, some people (including students) may expect you to have all the answers. Of course that's not possible, but you do have a wealth of resources at your disposal to help you as issues come up. The Bible is an invaluable tool for addressing life's problems and showing teens that they can trust Scripture to guide their ways. Keep this list of relevant Scriptures on key topics handy:

RELATIONSHIPS

"A friend loves at all times, and a brother is born for a time of adversity" (Prov. 17:17).

"Greater love has no one than this: to lay down one's life for one's friends" (John 15:13).

"Do not be yoked together with unbelievers. For what do righteousness and wickedness have in common? Or what fellowship can light have with darkness?" (2 Cor. 6:14).

Gen. 2:18; Gen. 2:24; Prov. 13:20; Prov. 18:24; Prov. 31:10–11; Mal. 1:6; Eph. 5:25; Heb. 10:24–25.

PARENTS

"Honor your father and your mother, so that you may live long in the land the LORD your God is giving you" (Ex. 20:12).

"Children, obey your parents in the Lord, for this is right. Honor your father and mother—which is the first commandment—with a promise so that it may go well with you and that you may enjoy long life on the earth" (Eph. 6:1–3).

"Fathers, do not embitter your children, or they will become discouraged" (Col. 3:20).

Lev. 19:3; Ps. 127:3–5; Ps. 139:13–16; Prov. 1:8–9; Prov. 22:6; Deut. 5:16; Mal. 1:6; Matt.18:12–14; Eph. 2:10.

SHARING YOUR FAITH

"Therefore go and make disciples of all nations, baptizing them in the name of the Father and of the Son and of the Holy Spirit" (Matt. 28:19).

"By this everyone will know that you are my disciples, if you love one another" (John 13:35).

"Jesus answered, 'I am the way and the truth and the life. No one comes to the Father except through me'" (John 14:6).

John 3:16; John 15:16; Acts 17:11; Rom. 1:12; Phil. 2:12–13; Phil. 1:6; 1 John 5:13.

TEMPTATION

"I have hidden your word in my heart that I might not sin against you" (Ps. 119:11).

"No temptation has overtaken you except what is common to mankind. And God is faithful; he will not let you be tempted beyond what you can bear. But when you are tempted, he will also provide a way out so that you can endure it" (1 Cor. 10:13).

"Blessed is a man who perseveres under trial; for once he has been approved, he will receive the crown of life which the Lord has promised to those who love Him. Let no one say when he is tempted, 'I am being tempted by God'; for God cannot be tempted by evil, and He Himself does not tempt anyone" (James 1:12–13).

Matt. 26:41; 1 Cor. 6:18; 1 Cor. 7:5; Eph. 6:11; Heb. 2:18; James 4:7.

ACCOUNTABILITY

"As iron sharpens iron, so one person sharpens another"
(Prov. 27:17).

"But the Advocate, the Holy Spirit, whom the Father will send
in my name, will teach you all things and will remind you of
everything I have said to you" (John 14:26).

"Have confidence in your leaders and submit to their authority,
because they keep watch over you as those who must give an
account. Do this so that their work will be a joy, not a burden,
for that would be of no benefit to you" (Heb. 13:17).

*Rom. 14:7–12; 1 Cor. 3:23; 1 Cor. 11:3; Eph. 4:11; Eph. 5:21; 1 Tim.
2:2; 1 Tim. 3:1–5; 1 Peter 5:2–3.*

FORGIVENESS

"Peter replied, 'Repent and be baptized, every one of you, in
the name of Jesus Christ for the forgiveness of your sins. And
you will receive the gift of the Holy Spirit'" (Acts 2:38).

"Blessed are those whose lawless deeds have been forgiven,
and whose sins have been covered. Blessed is the man whose
sin the Lord will not take account" (Rom. 4:7–8).

"If we confess our sins, he is faithful and just and will forgive us
our sins and purify us from all unrighteousness" (1 John 1:9).

Lev. 5:13; Matt. 6:12; Matt. 12:31; Matt. 26:28; Mark 1:4; Mark 3:28–29; Mark 4:12; Luke 1:77; Luke 7:47; John 20:23; Acts 13:38; Heb. 10:18; James 5:15; 1 John 2:12.

HEAVEN

"The LORD has established his throne in heaven, and his kingdom rules over all" (Ps. 103:19).

"May you be blessed by the LORD, the Maker of heaven and earth" (Ps. 115:15).

"Then I saw a new heaven and a new earth; for the first heaven and the first earth passed away, and there is no longer any sea. And I saw the holy city, new Jerusalem, coming down out of heaven from God, made ready as a bride adorned for her husband. And I heard a loud voice from the throne, saying, 'Behold, the tabernacle of God is among men, and He will dwell among them, and they shall be His people, and God Himself will be among them, and He will wipe away every tear from their eyes; and there will no longer beany death; there will no longer be any mourning, or crying, or pain; the first things have passed away" (Rev. 21:10–4).

Gen. 28:17; Ex. 20:4; Josh. 2:11; Judg. 13:20; 1 Kings 8:27; 2 Kings 19:15; 1 Chron. 21:16; Job 25:2; Ps. 69:34; Ps. 73:25; Ps. 124:8; Eccl. 3:1; Isa. 37:16; Matt. 3:2; Matt. 3:16; Matt. 5:10; Matt. 6:9; Matt. 6:19–20; Matt. 7:21; Mark 13:31; Luke 10:20; John 3:13;

Phil. 3:20; 1 Thess. 4:16; James 3:15; James 3:17; 2 Peter 3:13; Rev. 5:13; Rev. 11:12.

HELL

"Do not be afraid of those who kill the body but cannot kill the soul. Rather, be afraid of the One who can destroy both soul and body in hell" (Matt.10: 28).

"In Hades he lifted up his eyes, being in torment, and saw Abraham far away and Lazarus in his bosom. And he cried out and said, 'Father Abraham, have mercy on me, and send Lazarus so that he may dip the tip of his finger in water and cool off my tongue, for I am in agony in this flame.' But Abraham said, 'Child, remember that during your life you received your good things, and likewise Lazarus bad things; but now he is being comforted here, and you are in agony. And besides all this, between us and you there is a great chasm fixed, so that those who wish to come over from here to you will not be able, and that none may cross over from there to us'" (Luke 16:23–26).

"For if God did not spare angels when they sinned, but cast them into hell and committed them to pits of darkness, reserved for judgment; and did not spare the ancient world, but preserved Noah, a preacher of righteousness, with seven others, when He brought a flood upon the world of

the ungodly; and if He condemned the cities of Sodom
and Gomorrah to destruction by reducing them to ashes,
having made them an example to those who would live
ungodly lives thereafter; and if He rescued righteous Lot,
oppressed by the sensual conduct of unprincipled men (for
by what he saw and heard that righteous man, while living
among them, felt his righteous soul tormented day after day
by their lawless deeds), then the Lord knows how to rescue the
godly from temptation, and to keep the unrighteous under
punishment for the day of judgment" (2 Peter 2:4–9).

Matt. 5:22; Matt. 5:29; Luke 12:5; John 9:39; Rom. 2:2; James 3:6

SELF-ESTEEM

"For you formed my inward parts; you wove me in my
mother's womb. I will give thanks to You, for I am fearfully
and wonderfully made; Wonderful are Your works, and my
soul knows it very well" (Ps. 139:13–14).

"For we are God's handiwork, created in Christ Jesus to do
good works, which God prepared in advance for us to do"
(Eph. 2:10).

"How great is the love the Father has lavished on us, that we
should be called children of God! And that is what we are!"
(1 John 3:1).

Prov. 18:12; Mic. 6:8; Matt. 22:36–40; Luke 9:23; John 12:25;
1 Cor. 1:18–19; 1 Cor. 10:24; 2 Cor. 12:6–7; Eph. 4:2; Phil. 2:3;
2 Tim. 3:2–5; James 4:10.

LONELINESS

"No one will be able to stand against you all the days of your
life. As I was with Moses, so I will be with you; I will never
leave you nor forsake you" (Josh. 1:5).

"Be strong and courageous. Do not be afraid or terrified
because of them, for the LORD your God goes with you; he will
never leave you nor forsake you" (Deut. 31:6).

"Though my father and mother forsake me, the LORD will
receive me" (Ps. 27:10).

Is. 41:10; Is. 53:4; Ps. 23:5; Ps. 38:9; Matt. 11:28–29; Rom. 8:35–39;
1 Peter 5:7; 1 John 4:13.

GOD'S WILL

"Therefore I urge you, brethren, by the mercies of God, to
present your bodies a living and holy sacrifice, acceptable to
God, which is your spiritual service of worship. And do not be
conformed to this world, but be transformed by the renewing
of your mind, so that you may prove what the will of God is,
that which is good and acceptable and perfect" (Rom. 12:1–2).

"Trust in the LORD with all your heart. And do not lean on your own understanding. In all your ways acknowledge Him. And He will make your paths straight" (Prov. 3:5–6).

"If any of you lacks wisdom, you should ask God, who gives generously to all without finding fault, and it will be given to you" (James 1:5).

Jer. 19:11; Mic. 6:8; Matt. 6:10; Eph. 5:15–20; 1 Thess. 4:3; 1 Tim. 2:3–4; Heb. 10:36; Heb. 13:20–21; 1 Peter 2:15; 2 Peter 3:9.

APPENDIX B

QUICK-ACCESS GUIDE TO HELPFUL MINISTRIES, AGENCIES, AND ORGANIZATIONS

When issues arise that are beyond your expertise or you need to refer students to a professional, it's important to know where to go. Here is a list of ministries, agencies, and organizations that can help. (Also, spend some time getting to know your local agencies, as well, and add them to this list):

PHYSICAL OR SEXUAL ABUSE

National Teen Dating Abuse Helpline
(866) 331-9474 • loveisrespect.org

National Domestic Violence Hotline
(800) 799-SAFE • ndvh.org

Rape, Abuse, and Incest National Network
(800) 656-HOPE • rainn.org

BULLYING

National Center for Mental Health Promotion and Youth Violence Prevention
promoteprevent.org

Thursday's Child National Youth Advocacy Hotline
(800) USA-KIDS · thursdayschild.org

SELF-HARM

helpguide.org

parenting.org

webmd.com

SUICIDE

Christian Suicide Prevention
(888) 667-5947 · contact@christiansuicideprevention.com

National Hopeline Network
(800) SUICIDE · hopeline.com

EATING DISORDERS

National Association of Anorexia Nervosa and Eating Disorders
(630) 577-1330 · anad.org

National Eating Disorders Association
(800) 931-2237 • nationaleatingdisorders.org

DRUG ABUSE/ADDICTION

Al-Anon/Alateen
(888) 425-2666 • al-anon.alateen.org • index.php

National Institute on Alcohol Abuse & Alcoholism
(800) 662-HELP • niaaa.nih.gov

AT-RISK TEENS

Crisis Call Center
(800) 273-8255 • crisiscallcenter.org

TEEN PREGNANCY, ADOPTION SERVICES,
AND POST-ABORTION COUNSELING

PREGNANCY

Christian Life Resources
christianliferesources.com

Mercy Ministries
mercyministries.org

ADOPTION

Bethany Christian Services
bethany.org

A Act of Love Adoptions
aactofloveadoptions.com

POST-ABORTION COUNSELING

PATH (Post Abortion Treatment and Healing)
healingafterabortion.org

Project Rachel: Hope After Abortion
hopeafterabortion.org

Silent No More
silentnomoreawareness.org

APPENDIX C

QUICK-ACCESS GUIDE TO RESOURCES FOR WORKING WITH STUDENT MINISTRY VOLUNTEERS

In this section, I've provided several tools to assist you as you work with your student ministry volunteers.

1. VOLUNTEER LEADER EXPECTATIONS

It's a good idea to ask all volunteers to sign a statement indicating their commitment to the expectations outlined below:

As a volunteer, I am committing to:

1. Live a lifestyle of obedience to Christ.

2. Spend time daily in prayer and Bible reading.

3. Faithfully support the church.

4. Demonstrate a love for young people.

5. Abide by guidelines for interacting with students.

6. Abstain from activities that would compromise my character or could cause a student to stumble

(including, but not limited to, tobacco use, alcohol use, questionable entertainment, etc.).

7. Attend all student ministry events as outlined in my level of commitment.

8. Attend ongoing leadership training events.

9. Demonstrate a teachable spirit and a willingness to submit to authority.

10. Ongoing personal growth as a leader.

2. NEW LEADER ORIENTATION

At the beginning of each year, give volunteers specific guidelines to set them up to win and equip them to be effective leaders in the ministry.

1. The goal is to help students encounter God, connect with other students and find their place to serve.

2. Remember that services are like game day; you're there for the students, not to hang out with other leaders.

3. Be a thermostat rather than a thermometer; set the spiritual temperature for students by being passionate in worship, bringing your Bible, taking notes in service, etc.

4. Ask students about their involvement in upcoming events, helping them to see the bigger picture.

5. Always go out of your way to serve someone who is new, looks lost, or seems to be alone. Connect the student with an outgoing, mature student (preferably one who goes to the same school).

6. Sit with students in the services, not with other leaders; be prepared to confront students who may be a disruption.

7. Follow up with students after the service to help them process what they're learning.

8. Always support your leadership and/or peers when speaking to a student.

9. If a student is injured on church property, complete and submit an incident report before you leave.

10. Written parental permission is required for students to ride in a leader's car as part of an official church activity (including to and from small group meetings).

3. ESTABLISHING BOUNDARIES

Write out and distribute guidelines for establishing healthy boundaries between your leaders and students.

1. Remember that you're a student's leader first and their friend second.

2. Always under-promise and over-produce. If you make a promise, keep it.

3. Never be alone with a student of the opposite sex, and be wise about interaction with a student of the same gender.

4. Avoid inappropriate physical contact with a student (front hugs, shoulder rubs, corporal punishment, etc.).

5. Introduce yourself to a student's parents if you'll be spending time with them outside of church.

4. GUIDELINES FOR MENTORING STUDENTS

Offer specific insights for mentoring students effectively. Provide volunteers with specific information on the process for disciplining students.

1. Remember that only God can transform a life; the battle is won in prayer.

2. Remember that ministry flows out of relationship, and relationships take time.

3. Be a spiritual leader; always point students to Christ and to the Bible.

4. Be there for the important moments (times of crisis; birthdays; graduation; important games, plays, recitals, etc.) and make sure the student and their parents know you're there.

5. Remember that you are not the student's parent.

5. GUIDELINES FOR DISCIPLINING STUDENTS

Provide volunteers with specific information on the church's policy for disciplining students.

1. Remember that it's your responsibility to be prepared to appropriately discipline a student if needed.

2. Know that, to a teenager, ignoring an issue is the same as excusing it.

3. Never physically discipline a student.

4. Remember to take all factors into consideration when disciplining a student. You may discipline two students who did the same thing differently, depending on a variety of factors including circumstances, history, family background, etc.

5. Make sure the punishment matches the crime. Consult leadership for guidance.

6. Whenever you discipline a student, be sure to inform a staff member for your own protection.

7. Always involve a staff member if you feel a discipline situation is over your head—if you're not sure what to do, if someone has been hurt, or if a law has been broken.

6. CONNECTING WITH GUESTS

Use these guidelines to equip volunteers to interact with students new to the ministry and to help connect guests to other students, what's happening in the church, and to Christ.

1. **Make a positive impression:** You won't get a second chance at the first impression, so smile, make eye contact, and introduce yourself warmly. Tell the student you're glad they came.

2. **Don't forget their name:** Repeat the student's name a couple of times during the conversation so that you don't forget it. Remember that you may need to introduce them to someone else later.

3. **Keep the conversation moving:** If the student isn't talkative, be prepared to ask questions. Try to avoid ones that can lead to one-word answers (How did you hear about our youth ministry? What do you do for fun? What were you first impressions of our event tonight?)

4. **Listen carefully:** Be an active listener. Maintain eye contact. Don't be easily distracted. If you're interrupted by something during the conversation, apologize.

5. ***Look for common ground:*** As you talk, focus on the things you find you have in common (hobbies, friends, sports, etc.).

6. ***Talk about the church:*** The most obvious thing you have in common is a common place: the church. Mention upcoming church events.

7. ***Answer their questions:*** Ask students if they have any questions about the ministry, the church, or the service. If they do have questions, answer them helpfully. If you don't know the answer, excuse yourself and find an answer promptly.

8. ***Let them know what to expect:*** Remember that guests are in an unfamiliar environment. Help put them at ease by letting them know what they can expect through the rest of the service. ("We'll be going back into the service in a minute. We'll be going in during worship, where we'll be singing to say thank to God for all He's done for us.")

9. ***Make a connection:*** Connect guests with outgoing students who are their age. Ideal connections would be with students from their school, a nearby small group, or a student from a ministry team they're interested in. Be sure to connect the student; don't just pass

them off. If you aren't able to make a connection, offer to sit with the student if they're alone.

10. ***Follow-up:*** The next time you see students, call them by name and ask how they're doing.

ACKNOWLEDGEMENTS

This resource would not have been possible without the help of a great team. I'd like to thank Steve and Susan Blount and Lindy Lowry and Wendy Lee Nentwig for their valuable insight and editorial skills. Finally, a huge thanks to my incredible family for their patience and support during crazy seasons of ministry adventure.

ABOUT THE AUTHOR

Scotty Gibbons has been in youth ministry for more than twenty years and currently serves as the national youth strategist for the Assemblies of God National Leadership and Resource Center. He is the author of *Carry-On: Packing and Preserving for Success in Student Ministry; First Things First: A Devotional for Students;* and *Overflow: A Student's Guide to Living.*

Scotty loves doing life and ministry with his wife and best friend, Casey, and their six children, Candice, Kelly Grace, Bria, Allison, Angel, and Jordan.

For more information about Scotty Gibbons and his ministry, visit scottygibbons.com.

For more information about this book and other valuable resources visit www.salubrisresources.com